Employee Handbook

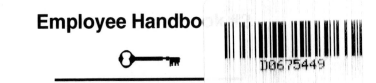

Discover the Key Basics of Life

"For Everyday Use at Work and Play"

The Simplicity
of
Systems Thinking

The Top 10 EVERYDAY Tools

From

Systems Thinking

Stephen Haines

Centre for Strategic Management®

Code HB-2 (Handbook #2) $9.95

CENTRE
FOR
STRATEGIC
MANAGEMENT®

Dear Systems Thinking Reader:

As a way to begin your progression to the "Systems Age," this Handbook is the second of four, outlining the concepts of Systems Thinking. You will find the tools you need to shift to a new, unique, and better way to think, act, and achieve results.

We recommend a one-day *Executive Briefing Session* with the Centre for Strategic Management® to help you get trained in Systems Thinking.

During this one day with your team, we will help you work through all 10 tools and their corresponding worksheets.

■ Use these tools every day at work on any task or project you are doing. Do it better!

■ Use these same tools every day at home or at play in your life.

Happy thinking...and acting...and better results!

Stephen Haines, President
Centre for Strategic Management®
San Diego, California
(619) 275-6528
www.csmintl.com

P.S.   To understand Systems Thinking fully, please ask us about our **Tool Kit and Reference Guide, Volume VIII on** *"Systems Thinking & Learning"* as well as our two other management books on the subject.

Check them out on our website:
www.SystemsThinkingPress.com

The Top 10 **EVERYDAY** Tools

From

Systems Thinking

"For **EVERYDAY** *Use at Work and Play"*

Focus on the Future!

"The future has always been difficult to
handle, so . . . it is really a challenge that
requires a broad input. Companies and
industries die because executives did not
think of what is yet to come."

—Adapted from P. Crosby

Discover the Key Basics of Life

TABLE OF CONTENTS

SECTION I: Overview of Our Systems Thinking Approach^{SM}

1. Thinking 8

2. Systems 13

3. Systems Thinking...16

4. Laws of Natural Systems 18

SECTION II: The Whole System

TOOL #1: Desired Outcomes 25

TOOL #2: Environmental Impacts 31

TOOL #3: Backwards Thinking 37

TOOL #4: Feedback is a Gift...43

TOOL #5: Helicopter View 49

SECTION III: The Inner Workings of All Living Systems

TOOL #6: Booster Shots 57

TOOL #7: Operational Flexibility 65

TOOL #8: Web of Relationships......................................71

TOOL #9: Root Causes..79

TOOL #10: Simplicity 85

SECTION IV: Information

About the Centre 92

About the Author...94

Ordering Information 95

The Simplicity of Systems Thinking

"For **EVERYDAY** *Use at Work and Play"*

SECTION I:

Overview
of
Systems Thinking

The Top 10 **EVERYDAY** Tools

From

Systems Thinking

Discover the Key Basics of Life

1. THINKING

Why Thinking Matters

The way you think creates the results you get. The most powerful way to impact the quality of your results is to improve the way you think.

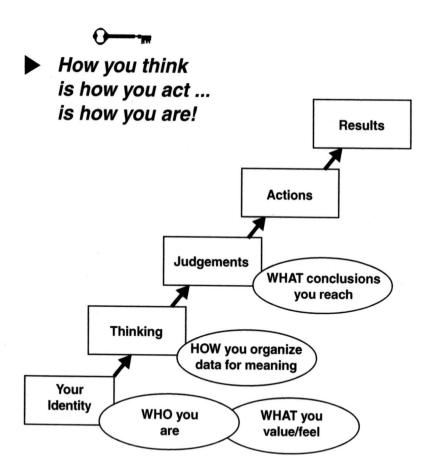

▶ *How you think is how you act ... is how you are!*

Results

Actions

Judgements — WHAT conclusions you reach

Thinking — HOW you organize data for meaning

Your Identity — WHO you are / WHAT you value/feel

"As ye thinketh, so shall ye be."

—*Jesus*

"Simply put, change our thoughts, and we can change our world."

—*Prem Chengalath, M.D.*

"The greatest discovery in our lives is that human beings, by changing the inner attitudes of their minds, *can change the outer aspects of their lives.*"

—*William James*

Thinking is Hard Work

"All the problems of the world could be settled easily if people were only willing to think.

The trouble is that people often resort to all sorts of devices in order not to think, *because thinking is such hard work.*"

—*Thomas J. Watson*

"If you think you can
...you're right.
If you think you can't
...you're right."

—*Henry Ford*

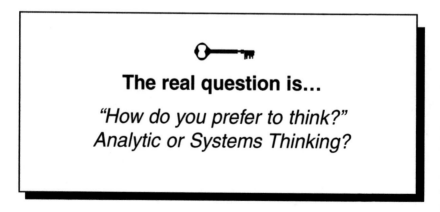

The real question is...

"How do you prefer to think?"
Analytic or Systems Thinking?

Analytical Thinking Gone Amuck!

"We've gone as far as we can with piecemeal Analytic Thinking." For Example:

1. IRS Rules—over 4,000 pages.

2. Health Care—thousands of small specialized entities based on singular type grants.

3. Social Services—thousands of small specialized entities based on singular categorical type grants.

4. Specialized Government Districts—water districts, assessment districts, school districts, etc.

5. Separate Cities and Counties—little or no geographic separation.

6. Federal Intelligence Agencies—16 of them.

7. Congressional Subcommittees—too numerous to count.

8. California—7,700 page education code.

9. U.S. Naval Academy regulations—from 10 to 1,000+ pages in 150 years.

10. Sears—29,000 pages of policies and procedures.

11. Federal Government Policies and Procedures— Al Gore's "Stacks and Stacks."

What else can you think of?

12. _____

13. _____

14. _____

Does this kind of control really work? What are the alternatives?

So we need to begin thinking differently!

Great Minds

Great Spirits have always encountered violent opposition from mediocre minds...

—*Albert Einstein*

Network of Mutuality
(not piecmeal)

"We are tied together in the single garment of destiny, caught in an inescapable network of mutuality."

—*Martin Luther King, Jr.*

This "mutuality" is called a System!

2. SYSTEMS

Systems Defined. . .
Systems are made up of a set of components that work together for the overall objectives of the whole (outputs).

Systems Thinking . . .
Is finding patterns and relationships, and learning to reinforce or change these patterns to fulfill your goals.

Systemic Change . . .
Is change that relates to or affects the entire family, department, or organization.

In Short . . .
The world can no longer be comprehended as a simple machine. It is a complex, highly interconnected system.

The Basic Trouble . . .
Is that most people are still trying to solve the problems of a complex system with the mentality and tools that were appropriate for the world as a . . .*Simple Machine.*

—*Ian Mitroff*

There are Many Types of Systems

There are many types and combinations of systems, which include:

1. **Mechanical/Electrical Systems**—cars, clocks, assembly lines

2. **Electronic Systems** (including Telecommunications)— PCs, LANs, WANs, supercomputers, Internet

3. **Ecological Systems**—21 Regions of North America (Sierra Club)

4. **Biological Systems**—birds, fish, animals, insects

5. **Human (Living) Systems**—individuals, teams, families, organizations, communities

Open Systems vs. Closed Systems

Systems can be considered in two ways: closed or open. While they are difficult to defend in the absolute, **the concept of relatively open or relatively closed systems is important.**

Open vs. Closed Systems

More Closed ← Relatively → More Open

Any system isolated from its environment is called a closed system. One that receives inputs from the environment and/ or acts on the environment through outputs is called an open system.

Open Systems are Living Systems

Systems as Universal Laws or Principles

"You can't cheat Mother Nature"

A Simple Analogy: Farmers know natural systems are governed by principles. There is a rhythm and cycle to the seasons of the year—planting and harvesting must follow this rhythm in order to be successful.

Other Universal Laws

- The lifecycle of "birth, growth, maturity, decline, death" of all living things (people, plants, animals, birds, fish)
- The food chain—on land and in water
- 24 hours in a day
- **■** Balance of nature (i.e., deer/wolves)
- Four seasons
- 365 days in a year
- **■** Gravity
- Male/female roles in procreation
- Wind/fire and sun/moon
- **■** Land, water, air
- **■** Things get worse before they get better
- **■** To survive as human beings we need physical, social, emotional, mental, and spiritual stimulation and nourishment

If you're not living in harmony with the natural laws and principles of the universe (earth), you won't be as satisfied or be as successful.

—*Stephen Haines*

3. SYSTEMS THINKING

A Better Language (and Way of Being)

Systems Thinking principles are like a wide-angle lens on a camera. They give you a better view on your "radar scope" and thus **a more effective way of thinking, communicating, problem solving, and acting!**

▶ *Otherwise: "Today's analytic and piecemeal thinking (and problem solving) is the source of tomorrow's problems."*

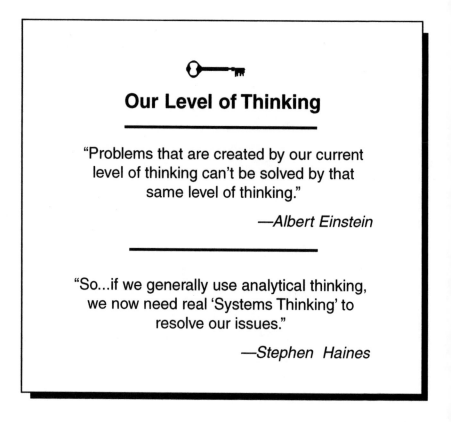

Our Level of Thinking

"Problems that are created by our current level of thinking can't be solved by that same level of thinking."

—*Albert Einstein*

"So...if we generally use analytical thinking, we now need real 'Systems Thinking' to resolve our issues."

—*Stephen Haines*

Analytic vs. Systems Thinking

The dominant view in our lives is "Analytic Thinking," as we saw. However, the **Natural Order of the Universe and Life** is a *Systems* one. Analytic approaches (and analytic thinking) to systems problems is *bankrupt* in our society and organizations!

The good news is that this new "Systems Thinking View" is beginning to emerge—witness the increased use of systems-oriented words such as:

- United
- Fit
- Integration
- Collaboration
- Cooperation
- Teamwork
- Partnerships
- Alliances
- Linkages
- Stakeholders
- Wholistic
- Seamless
- Boundaryless
- System
- Synergistic

This opens up whole new vistas and THE newly emerging paradigm that is a better fit with reality . . . and the *Natural Order of the Universe and Life.*

And...it is the Laws of the Natural Systems on Earth that have been re-discovered.

○━━▅

Discovery

"Discovery consists in seeing what
everyone else has seen and thinking what
no one else has thought."

—*Albert Szent-Gyorgi*

4. Laws of Natural Systems

Natural Laws (Systems)	vs	Standard Human Dynamics (Analytic)

I. THE WHOLE SYSTEM: "The whole is greater than the sum of its parts."

1. Wholism:
- ■ Overall Broader Perspectives
- Purpose-Focused
- Synergy, Ends

2. Open Systems:
- ■ Open to Environment
- Regular Scanning
- "Outside-in"
- Implications

3. Boundaries:
- Clarity of Systems
- Integrated Fit
- Collaborative
- Complimentary

4. Input/Output:
- How Natural Systems Operate
- "Backwards Thinking"

5. Feedback:
- On Effectiveness
- ■ Results
- "Feedback is a Gift"
- Encourage It

6. Multiple Outcomes:
- Goal Seeking at All Levels
- ■ WIFM

1. Parts-Focused:
- ■ Suboptimal Results
- ■ Narrower Views
- ■ Means-Focused

2. Closed Systems:
- ■ Low Environmental Scanning or Concern
- ■ Parts-Focused

3. Fragmented:
- ■ Turf Battles
- ■ Voids
- ■ Overlaps
- ■ Duplication

4. Sequential:
- ■ Linear
- ■ Mechanistic
- ■ Piecemeal, Analytic
- ■ Forecasts

5. Low Feedback
- ■ Financial Only
- ■ Defensiveness
- ■ Lack of Measures

6. Conflict:
- ■ Artificial "Either/Or" Thinking
- ■ "Yes, but..."
- ■ One Best Way

Natural Laws (Systems)	vs	Standard Human Dynamics (Analytic)

II. THE INNER WORKINGS: Synergy, integration, and interdependence

7. Equifinality:
- ■ Flexibility
- ■ Adaptive
- ☐ Outcome-Focused
- ■ Empower Means

8. Entropy:
- ☐ Follow-up
- ☐ Inputs of Energy
- ☐ Renewal
- ■ Booster Shots

9. Hierarchy:
- ☐ Flatter Organization
- ☐ Self-Organizing
- ☐ Order Emerges

10. Interrelated Parts:
- ■ Patterns
- ■ Interdependence
- ☐ Leverage and Fit
- ☐ Involvement and Participation
- ☐ Web of Relationships

11. Dynamic Equilibrium:
- ■ Maintain Stability, Balance, and Culture
- ■ Self-Regulating (disequilibrium on the edge)

12. Internal Elaboration:
- ☐ Details and Sophistication
- ☐ Clarity and Simplicity

7. Direct Cause-Effect:
- ■ One Best Way
- ■ Quick Fix Fails
- ■ Activity-Focused

8. Decline:
- ■ Rigidity
- ■ Obsolete
- ■ Death

9. Bureaucracy:
- ■ Command, Control
- ■ Hierarchy
- ■ Policies Paramount
- ■ Centralized

10. Separate Parts:
- ■ Components
- ■ Entities
- ■ Silos
- ■ Individualism
- ■ Parts are Primary

11. Resistance to Change:
- ■ Short-Term Myopic View
- ■ Ruts
- ■ Habits
- ■ Root Causes Delayed in Time and Space

12. Complexity:
- ■ Confusion
- ■ Chaos

A Basic Reorientation of
Our Thinking is Needed

"In one way or another, we are forced to deal with complexities, with 'wholes' or 'systems' in all fields of knowledge. This implies a basic reorientation in scientific thinking.

—*Ludwig Van Bertalanffy*
(Father of Systems Thinking)

IN SUMMARY

"If life on earth is governed by the natural laws of living systems, then a successful participant should learn the rules."

—*Stephen Haines*

Thus:

The Systems Thinking Approach[SM] **is an absolute necessity to succeed in today's complex world.**

—*Stephen Haines*

The Simplicity of Systems Thinking

"For Everyday Use at Work and Play"

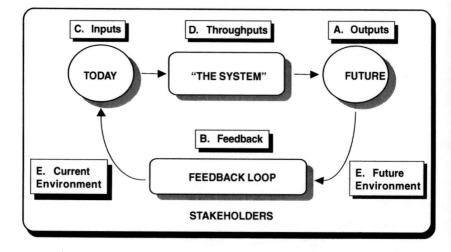

"From Complexity to Simplicity"

SECTION II:

The Whole System

The Top 10 EVERYDAY Tools

From

Systems Thinking

Discover the Key Basics of Life

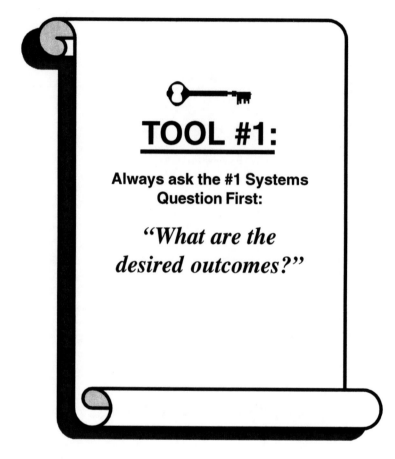

TOOL #1:

Always ask the #1 Systems Question First:

"What are the desired outcomes?"

TOOL #1: Desired Outcomes

> **Always ask the #1 Systems Question First:**
> *"What are the desired outcomes?"*

Since systems usually have multiple outcomes, this is a more complex question than at first glance.

PRINCIPLE

> **Living systems here on earth (ie., people) are naturally goal-seeking.**

No matter what you do all day long at work or at play, it is of tremendous value to develop clarity and agreement on your desired outcomes *before* beginning any actions.

Keep in mind, there are usually multiple outcomes—not *"either/or"* responses from reductionistic thinking.

Other words for OUTCOMES include:

- Vision
- Mission
- Results
- Ends
- Purpose
- Destination
- Objectives
- Goal
- Outputs

Without agreement on the ends from the people who matter, our actions rarely have a chance of succeeding.

Once the desired outcome (the "what") is clear in our lives, there are many ways (the "how") to arrive at this destination.

Know Your Destination First!

What's Your Target?

Success

"The great successful men (and women) of the world have used their imagination. They think ahead and create their mental picture, and then go to work materializing that picture in all its details, filling in here, adding a little there, altering this a bit and that a bit, but steadily building—steadily building."

—*Robert Collier*

EXAMPLES

▶ We usually are reasonably sure of our destination (desired outcome) before we begin driving our car.

By the same token, a project manager would not begin a project without knowing the project goals. However, we often run our businesses, jobs, and lives without clearly knowing our desired outcomes.

▶ Organizational outcomes often include what can be called a "Triple-Bottom-Line" composed of:

    1) the needs of customers, and

    2) the needs of employees, and

    3) the needs of stockholders.

A "Triple-Double" would also include the needs of:

    4) the community, and

    5) suppliers, as well.

Thinking about your "Triple-Bottom-Line" is the beginning of "Backwards Thinking" (or, thinking backwards from your "desired destination" in order to figure out how to achieve it—see Tool #3).

▶ For every organizational task, there are at least two desired outcomes—the organization's and the individual's. Each of us has a permanent sign across our chest of WIIFM ("What's In It For Me?").

▶ Do you have clear destinations for yourself, your family, and your children? Or are you like most people—just living your life day to day?

Further, "desired outcomes" are all about setting goals. In all the literature, the #1 criteria for success is goal setting (so be sure to establish your vision or purpose).

EXAMPLES

▶ In simplistic and personal terms, it means making a daily "action" list so you focus on actions that lead to the results you want, not just talk and good ideas.

▶ Many meetings are a waste of time. If you want to make any meeting in your life more effective—just ask the #1 Systems Question: What are the desired outcomes from this meeting?

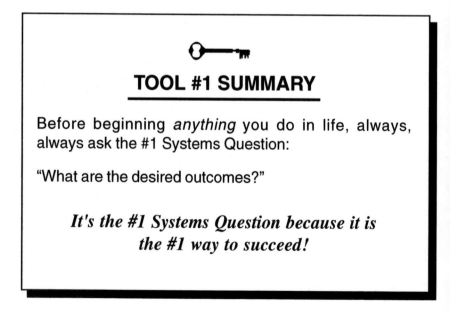

TOOL #1 SUMMARY

Before beginning *anything* you do in life, always, always ask the #1 Systems Question:

"What are the desired outcomes?"

It's the #1 Systems Question because it is the #1 way to succeed!

Worksheet #1

I. At Work

What are my three main objectives in my job:

A) For the next three months:

   1. _____

   2. _____

   3. _____

B) For the next year:

   1. _____

   2. _____

   3. _____

II. At Play & Life

What are my (or my family's) top three goals:

A) For the next year:

   1. _____

   2. _____

   3. _____

B) For the next five years:

   1. _____

   2. _____

   3. _____

NOTE: See our website at www.SystemsThinkingPress.com for our ***Strategic Career and Life Planning*** book and workbook to look more deeply into this subject.

TOOL #2:

Environmental Impact

"What will be changing in the environment that will impact us?"

TOOL #2: Environmental Impact

> **Keep asking The Systems Question:**
> *"What will be changing in the environment that will impact us?"*

In today's rapidly changing environment, people and organizations who fail to constantly scan their environment to see what is changing are unlikely to be successful.

EXAMPLES

▶ In organizational terms, the acronym "SKEPTIC" is one framework to use. It includes scanning for changes in the environment in your:

S	— Socio-Demographics (People/Population)
K	— "K"ompetition (British spelling)
E	— Economics/Environment itself
P	— Political/Regulatory
T	— Technology
I	— Industry, and, of course, your
C	— Customers or Clients

▶ In individual terms, it means paying attention to changes in the environment that may impact all the roles one plays in life, such as "PITO."

P	— Personally: body, mind, spirit
I	— Interpersonally: family, friends, colleagues
T	— Team: associations, communities, departments
O	— Organization: job, career, wealth, enjoyment, and satisfaction

Scan Your Environment

"Scan-Focus-Act"

—*Andrew Papageorge*

PRINCIPLE

*Align change from the outside-in—
not the inside-out.*

Employ "Backwards Thinking:"

Start with the future environment. Scan it for trends and the wants and needs of yourself and your customers. Then define your desired outcomes. Only then do you work backwards to determine "how to" meet these outcomes.

Align the entire organization, across all departments, to meet the defined outcomes. This is the conceptual basis for TQM (Total Quality Management) and business process reengineering in today's organizations. However, it is often fragmented into departmental elements or limited only to internal cost-cutting activities—without regard to customer impact.

USES

▶ **For Organizations:** Set up a full Environmental Scanning System by assigning responsibility to collect data on future environmental trends that may impact you. Assign each letter of SKEPTIC to a leader and team with a passion for this area.

▶ Conduct Quarterly Environmental Scanning Sessions where everyone shares his or her trends and deduces impacts on your organization as a result.

▶ Revise your Strategic Plan yearly with this as a key input.

▶ **For Teams, Departments, and Units:** Select the key SKEPTIC aspects that most affect your field and focus on those instead of the entire range. However, keep in mind that most futurist experts believe that the key environmental trend to watch is technology, as it drives all else.

USES

▶ **For Families:** Are all family members becoming conversant with technology today, especially the internet and e-mail? What about cell phones? These communications devices allow us cheap (almost free) world-wide, instantaneous communications.

▶ **Personally:** Keep yourself open to what is changing in the environment—not just through the typical media, but through other means as well (such as magazines and newsletters, especially in your field). Note trends and directions related to your hobbies as well.

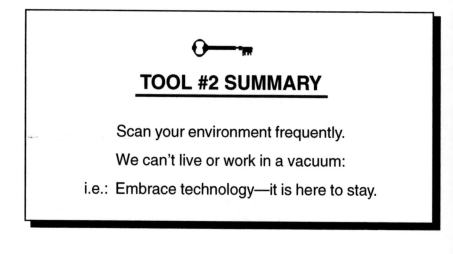

TOOL #2 SUMMARY

Scan your environment frequently.

We can't live or work in a vacuum:

i.e.: Embrace technology—it is here to stay.

Worksheet #2

I. At Work

In my job, what are three key environmental trends I need to react and adjust to:

A) In the next six months:

  1. _____

  2. _____

  3. _____

B) In the next 3-5 years:

  1. _____

  2. _____

  3. _____

II. At Play & Life

In my personal life, what are the three key environmental trends that I need to react and adjust to:

A) In the next six months:

  1. _____

  2. _____

  3. _____

B) In the next 3-5 years:

  1. _____

  2. _____

  3. _____

TOOL #3:

"Backwards Thinking"

"What is impossible to do today, but if it could be achieved, would fundamentally change what we are?"

TOOL #3: "Backwards Thinking"

> **The Ideal Vision Question:**
> *"What is impossible to do today, but if it could be achieved, would fundamentally change what we are?"*

This tool is a simple visual summary of Tools #1 through #6, integrating them into a mental picture that is easy to remember.

The integrated Systems Thinking **A-B-C-D-E** visual drawing below represents a **"New Orientation to Life."**

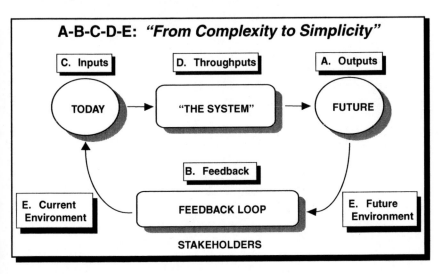

It Asks First:
A Where do you ideally want to be (Desired Outcomes)?

Then, Backwards Thinking:
B How will you know you've gotten there (Feedback is a Gift)?

C Where are you now (Today's Issues and Problems)?

D How do you get there (Close the gap from C →A)?

And, Ongoing:
E What may change in your environment in the future?

Banff, the Canadian Rockies

The Earth is a Natural Living System

There are 21 natural ecosystems in North America that have natural inputs and outputs with their environment.

These natural ecosystems are not only peaceful and beautiful but are essential to preserve the future of life on earth as we know it.

Systems Thinking vs. Analytic Thinking

Analytic Thinking:

1. Starts with today and the current state, issues, and problems.
2. Breaks the issues into their smallest components.
3. Solves each component separately.
4. Has no far reaching ideal vision or goal (except for the goal of the absence of the problem).

Note:

In Systems Thinking, the whole is primary and the parts are secondary.

In Analytic Thinking, the parts are primary and the whole is secondary.

▶ *"If you don't know where you're going, any road will get you there."*

EXAMPLES

▶ In the world of work, many of us get up each day, go to work, and work very hard. But do we have a game plan for an "Ideal Future Vision" of where we want to be in a few years? Very rarely. In our western society technical schools (such as science, engineering, finance, law), we are taught to think from today forward, incrementally to the future, not vice versa.

▶ We also rarely get a chance to see the whole picture at work—often our jobs aren't designed for that. We work hard on our part of the organization on the assumption that if each of us does our best, the organization will thrive.

▶ While hard-working, competent employees are necessary for success, they are not sufficient. In Backwards Thinking, you start with the future, define its ideal, and only then do you try to fit all the parts of the system together to support each other.

39

EXAMPLE

▶ In our personal lives, we read left to right, we focus on today's activities and our small location of the world. Is it any wonder that most of us are excellent left-brained, analytical thinkers?

The more right-brained, wholistic, and strategic thinkers are few and far between. For, Systems Thinking and Strategic Thinking are the same.

⚬━ᴍ
TOOL #3 SUMMARY

So, in reality for most people in western society, this tool with its **A-B-C-D-E** methodology represents a **New Orientation to Life**.

It sounds simple, but the rest of society focuses on the parts first and not the whole.

Worksheet #3

I. At Work

If you could change the most important one or two things in your world of work and career, what would it be (no matter what the cost or effort)?

A) In the next six months:

1. _____

2. _____

B) In the next three years:

1. _____

2. _____

Now work "Backwards" to make them a reality.

II. At Play and Life

If you could change the most important one or two things in your personal life, what would it be (no matter what the cost or effort)?

A) In the next six months:

1. _____

2. _____

B) In the next three years:

1. _____

2. _____

Now work "Backwards" to make them a reality.

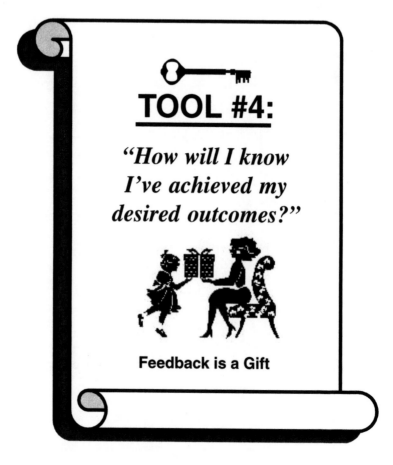

TOOL #4:

*"How will I know
I've achieved my
desired outcomes?"*

Feedback is a Gift

TOOL #4: Feedback is a Gift

> **The Systems Question:**
> *"How will I know I've achieved my desired outcomes?"*

The concept of feedback is important in understanding how a living (human) system maintains a steady state, or, alternatively, how we can change successfully. Information concerning the outputs of our system are fed back as an input to our system so that we may make corrections and maintain a steady-state (if that is our goal).

This crucial concept, taken from the *Control Theory of Engineering*, consists of modifying the behavior of any living (human) system by reinserting the results of actual past performance.

Feedback can be negative or positive. While positive feedback gives you the input that no adjustment is necessary in order to reach your desired outcomes, negative feedback is informa-tion which indicates that the system is deviating from a prescribed course and must adjust or the desired outcomes will not be achieved.

So, negative feedback is good! In fact, it is a personal and business "survival skill" to use in today's rapidly changing environment.

Regular Check-ups are Key:

Both At Work and At Play!

EXAMPLES

▶ In most teams and organizations, there is very little feedback ever offered or received. On the other hand, the importance of feedback and regular check-ups is natural in our lives. Consider:

Car Maintenance:
- Mechanic/Hood
- Gasoline
- Preventive Maintenance

Personal Health:
- Annual Physical
- Exercise
- Proper Eating

Training Camp or Pre-Season Practice:
- Intense Preparation
- Study and Performance
- Evaluation of Players

Instead of Feedback, With a Problem, we:
- Ignore It
- Work Harder
- Splinter into factions
- Get Out

PRINCIPLE

Feedback is the breakfast of champions. Be flexible and adaptive.

In today's complex and continually changing world, in order to achieve your desired outcomes, initial solutions are not as important as the ability to gain constant feedback and adapt.

The ability to be flexible and adaptive (i.e., to learn, grow, change and adapt to changes in the environment) is crucial. Economies of speed are replacing economies of scale as a key competitive edge. Feedback is the key so that we can learn, grow, and adapt at all levels of the organizational system (individuals, teams, and the organization).

EXAMPLE

▶ Feedback is a gift—allow others to give it to you! It is the skill of being open and receptive to (and even encouraging) feedback from your customers, your employees, your supervisor, and peers. Ask *anyone* who can help you to learn and grow as a person and human being, as a professional, and as a leader of your organization. Ask your parents, children, and friends, as well.

The Corollary Question is—*How do you develop self-mastery?* How to develop the external *style* and *inner psyche* to genuinely encourage others to help you with this *gift* of feedback, even when it *hurts.*

▶ *Be open to learning, even if painful.*

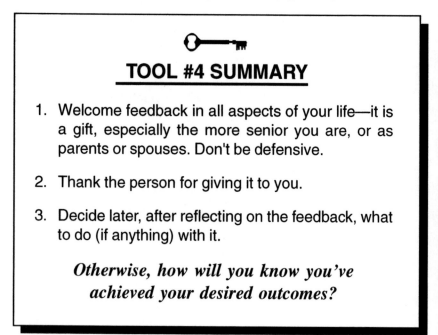

TOOL #4 SUMMARY

1. Welcome feedback in all aspects of your life—it is a gift, especially the more senior you are, or as parents or spouses. Don't be defensive.

2. Thank the person for giving it to you.

3. Decide later, after reflecting on the feedback, what to do (if anything) with it.

Otherwise, how will you know you've achieved your desired outcomes?

Worksheet #4

I. At Work

A) What are your strengths and weaknesses at work? Feedback is a gift—encourage others to give it to you. Whom do you trust to give honest, caring feedback? List them here and ask them for feedback:_____

1. _____

2. _____

3. _____

B) What feedback do you need, and are not now getting, in regards to your job performance? List it here:

1. _____

2. _____

3. _____

II. At Play and Life

A) What is your relationship to your family and close friends? List those who you can trust to give you honest (and caring) feedback:

1. _____

2. _____

3. _____

B) What three questions will you ask them?

1. _____

2. _____

3. _____

TOOL #5:

Helicopter View

*"What is our common
higher level
(superordinate) goal?"*

The Ultimate Systems Question

TOOL #5: Helicopter View

(Common Goals)

> **The Ultimate Systems Question:**
> *"What is our common higher level (superordinate) goal?"*

Common Higher Level (Superordinate) Goals

As Einstein said, "Problems can't be solved at the level they were created," so go to the next higher level in order to succeed. Focus on abundance (win-win) vs. scarcity (win-lose) goals through the use of higher systems order outcomes.

"To raise new questions, new possibilities,
to regard old problems from a new angle,
requires creative imagination and marks
a real advance in science."

—*Albert Einstein*

PRINCIPLE

The Ultimate Systems Principle:
"Problems can't be solved at the
level they were created."
—Albert Einstein

Take a Helicopter View of Life!

Gain a Better Perspective

We must learn to see the world anew."

—*Albert Einstein*

"So ... if we generally use analytical thinking in our lives, we now need real 'Systems Thinking' to resolve our issues."

—*Stephen Haines*

Helicopter View

We can't all get into a space shuttle but we can all get into a helicopter and have the pilot rise to 7000 feet and "hover" to help us get a better perspective on our issues and problems (as well as opportunities). The ability to adopt this *"helicopter view"* is what:

■ Finds common goals and common ground to work with.

■ Finds better answers and solutions to problems— especially "third alternatives."

■ Helps us become a better systems and strategic thinker.

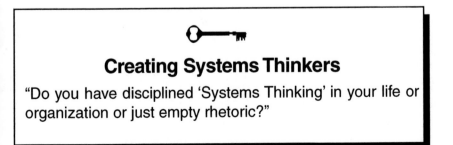

Creating Systems Thinkers

"Do you have disciplined 'Systems Thinking' in your life or organization or just empty rhetoric?"

EXAMPLES

▶ In union-management fights and strikes over pay, it is a win-lose game. By moving to the higher level goal of competing and selling more cars profitably, both sides can win by gaining more money (increasing the size of the pie).

▶ In your day-to-day life, do you think about your future vision and your highest level goals?

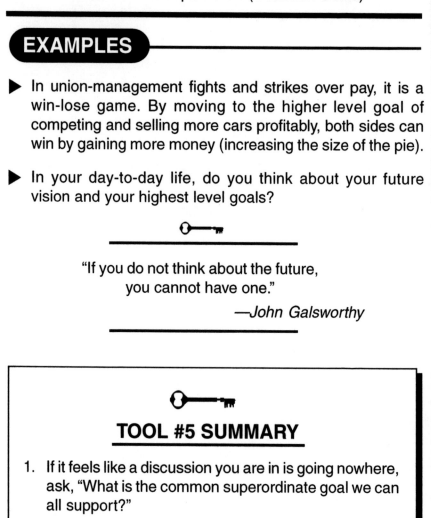

"If you do not think about the future,
you cannot have one."

—*John Galsworthy*

TOOL #5 SUMMARY

1. If it feels like a discussion you are in is going nowhere, ask, "What is the common superordinate goal we can all support?"

2. In planning your day, week, month, or year, ask "What is the common higher (superordinate) goal we can all support?" Sometimes this is seen as a "Shared Vision."

3. As a way to a higher goal, you may want to ask both sides involved in a conflict, "Is there a third alternative in which we both can win?"

Worksheet #5

I. At Work

Think of someone whom you do not get along with at work, but with whom you'd like to improve your relationship. List the person here (or initials for confidentiality): _____

A) Can you think of one or two common goals you both share?

1. _____

2. _____

B) What initial steps can you take to build a better relationship with them, using the one or two common goals as a reference point?

1. _____

2. _____

3. _____

I. At Play & Life

Think of someone whom you do not get along with at work, but with whom you'd like to improve your relationship. List the person here (or initials for confidentiality): _____

A) Can you think of one or two common goals you both share?

1. _____

2. _____

B) What initial steps can you take to build a better relationship with them, using the one or two common goals as a reference point?

1. _____

2. _____

3. _____

The Simplicity of Systems Thinking

"For Everyday Use at Work and Play"

The Inner Workings of a System are Complex

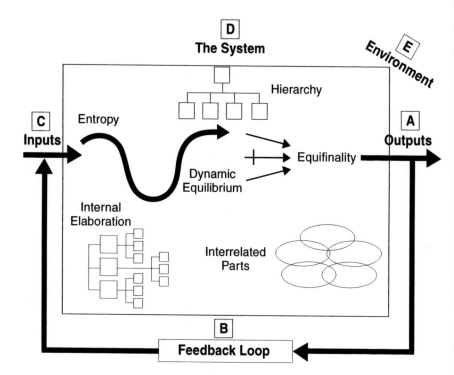

How do we create simplicity out of complexity?

SECTION III:

"The Inner Workings"
(Of All Living Systems)

The Top 10 **EVERYDAY** Tools

From

Systems Thinking

Discover the Key Basics of Life

TOOL #6:

Booster Shots

"What do we need to do to ensure buy-in and stay-in over time?"

*Reverse the Entropy—
Get a Booster Shot!*

TOOL #6: Booster Shots

Systems Question:

"What do we need to do to ensure buy-in and stay-in over time?"

In every situation we face in life, there is an entropy process occurring (the normal tendency of a system to run down and deteriorate over time), just like a car running low on fuel or the nourishment needs of your body. We need to focus continually on reversing this entropy with booster shots. "Buy-in" isn't the killer of change—it's the lack of "stay-in" over time.

Entropy Defined: All problems conform to the laws of inertia—the longer you wait, the harder the problem is to correct. Entropy is the tendency for any system to run down and eventually become inert.

Incremental Degradation: The main barrier to achieving the "fit" of all organization processes and actions with the desired values and vision is incremental degradation, where the parts wear out, bit by bit, due to lack of new energy.

In order to be effective, any system requires continual attention, booster shots, stop checks, etc. on a regular basis.

PRINCIPLE

Reverse the Entropy!
Give Booster Shots.

Systems can continuously increase in complexity until they become very bureaucratic and ossified, ultimately resulting in the death of the system. All living systems require constant energy if they are to reverse this entropy process. Otherwise, all living systems eventually run down and die.

In addition, we now have a virtually limitless supply of constant feedback, which provides us with new input toward change—this is the good news in our worldwide instantaneous information transmissions.

Booster Rockets

"Booster Shots" are required for the space shuttle to reach orbit

Signs of Organizational Entropy
From: *New Management* by Max DePree, CEO, Herman Miller

- A tendency toward superficiality.

- A dark tension among key people.

- No longer have time for celebration and ritual.

- A recurring effort by some to convince others that business is, after all, quite simple. (The acceptance of complexity and ambiguity and the ability to deal with them constructively is essential.)

- When problem-makers outnumber problem-solvers.

- When folks confuse heroes with celebrities.

- When leaders seek to control rather than liberate.

- When the pressure of day-to-day operations pushes aside our concern for vision and risk.

- An orientation toward the dry rules of business school rather than a value orientation which takes into account such things as contribution, spirit, excellence, beauty, and joy.

- When people speak of customers as impositions on their time rather than as opportunities to serve.

- When manuals grow in size.

- When leaders rely on structures instead of people.

- When a loss of grace and style and civility occurs.

- When a loss of respect for the English language occurs.

Building a Critical Mass for Change

1. It can take one to two years to build critical mass for large scale change. The following are ways to help you do this:

    ■ Modify Change Plan drafts — listen, review (share and gain feedback) from those affected.

    ■ Continue to hold meetings with key stakeholders throughout implementation.

    ■ Develop trust in your leadership by being open via a Change Leadership Steering Committee — involve skeptics and listen to them every day.

2. Develop Annual Plans for all departments, divisions, and sections under the Strategic Plan/core strategy umbrella.

3. Create "updates" after each Change Steering Committee meeting and ask for feedback.

4. Use Strategy Sponsorship Teams as "change agents" for each core strategy or major change.

5. Implement quick changes or actions so people know you are serious (silent majority).

6. Review reward systems and the performance appraisal form to reinforce core values and core strategies.

7. Answer WIIFM ("What's In It For Me") for each person looking at political and cultural issues.

> Remember: **"Skeptics are our best friends."**
>
> If you encounter skeptics, be sure to ask them why they are skeptical. Get them to identify the roadblocks. Don't try to force them to agree with you.

Ways to Institutionalize Desired Changes

"Stay-In" year after year requires **institutionalizing the desired changes.** Some ways to do this include:

1. Conduct refresher training courses/yearly conferences on the change topic.
2. Conduct a reward system's diagnosis and ensure that the rewards are consistent with the changes.
3. Have ways to discuss and reinforce the change at staff, team and group meetings.
4. Use a variety of communication avenues and processes for both one-way and two-way feedback on the change.
5. Set up a process of yearly renewing and reexamining the change in order to continually improve it.
6. Look closely at the key environmental factors to be sure they are reinforcing the changes.
7. Create physical indications of the permanency of the change (offices, jobs, brochures, etc.).
8. Link other organizational systems to the change. Encourage specific communications between them.
9. Keep the goals and benefits of the change clear and well known.
10. Be alert to other changes that can negatively affect this change (unintended negative consequences).
11. Have one person manage the change (the change agent) and a different person manage the stability (the stay agent). Change agents are poor stay agents!

EXAMPLE

▶ While human beings and families obviously have a finite life cycle, it doesn't have to be this way for neighborhoods, communities, and organizations. For them, the renewal process that reverses entropy is key to long-term success. As Margaret Wheatley discusses in her recent book *Leadership and the New Science*, chaos and disorder can lead to renewal and growth at a higher level.

EXAMPLES

▶ From a personal point of view, humans experience the same natural phenomenon as systems of running down and dying. If you want your career to progress, you need to focus on constant new learning, reinforcement, and adaption of existing knowledge.

In addition, you need to embrace technology and all the changes it represents. From a business perspective, almost every job in every organization has been changed as a result of technological advances.

▶ Our personal lives have also been affected by the speed and pace of change in our lives, often called "Internet time." Because of this barrage of information, real learning often requires us to hear something three or four times (repetition, repetition, repetition).

The same is true with our children who are constantly bombarded with media stimuli. They require **"Booster Shots"** and reminders (repetition, repetition, repetition), which can be helpful in all aspects of their lives.

TOOL #6 SUMMARY

All projects, systems and new changes have a tendency to run down and die over time.

THUS: Check-ups, Follow-ups, and Booster Shots are key to success!

Worksheet #6

I. At Work

Think of something new you have recently implemented that is important to you. List it: _____

_____

Now, you know it will run down in its effectiveness over time, so what kind of Booster Shots or Actions will you need to ensure longer term successful implementation?

Actions/Boosters: **How Frequent:**

1. _____   _____

2. _____   _____

3. _____   _____

II. At Play & Life

Think of someone important to you in your life— like someone living far away from you. List the person: _____

_____

Now, list 3 - 5 Booster Shots or Actions you will need to maintain that relationship at its highest level.

Actions/Boosters: **How Frequent:**

1. _____   _____

2. _____   _____

3. _____   _____

4. _____   _____

5. _____   _____

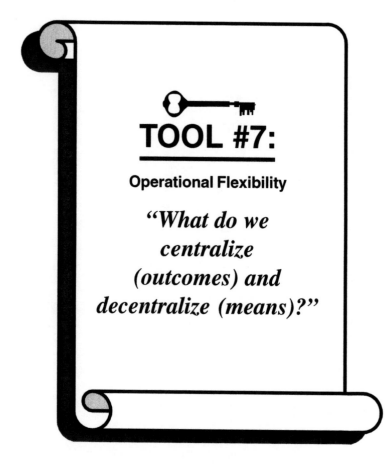

TOOL #7:

Operational Flexibility

"What do we centralize (outcomes) and decentralize (means)?"

The 21st Century Truism:

Strategic Consistency & Operational Flexibility

TOOL #7: Operational Flexibility

Strategic Consistency & Operational Flexibility

> **Key Systems Question:**
> *"What do we centralize (outcomes) and what should we decentralize (means)?"*

In today's world, it is key to build strategic consistency (the "what") while maintaining operational flexibility (the "how"). Focus on what is strategic and what is operational.

"Either/or" questions, such as centralize vs. decentralize, are too simplistic today. One size no longer fits all. Consistency isn't always the answer, especially in the "how to" arena.

Strategic consistency (the "what") to your vision and operational flexibility (the "how") are the successors to the centralize vs. decentralize dilemma of most organizations.

PRINCIPLE

There are many different ways to achieve the same desired outcomes. Thus, the key is to ensure the right people are involved in planning and implementing the solution.

In operations...

Speed is of the essence!

EXAMPLE ————————————————

▶ Organizations need both better strategic consistency and more operational flexibility in today's fast-paced world.

"People support what they help create."

It follows that decision-making should be as close as possible to the actions (and the system or entity we desire to change). People have a natural desire to be involved and provide input into decisions that affect them *before* the decision is made. For leaders, this is called participatory management skills.

EXAMPLE ————————————————

▶ Today's perspective requires a different way of looking at organizations in this new fashion. It requires a much higher level of wisdom and maturity not to abdicate or to be *"all controlling"* but to find the middle ground of interdependence.

The **Third Level of Maturity** is required for this interdependence and flexibility to work best.

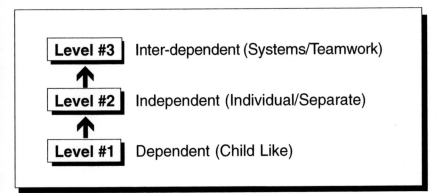

Level #3	Inter-dependent (Systems/Teamwork)
Level #2	Independent (Individual/Separate)
Level #1	Dependent (Child Like)

EXAMPLES

- **Whether in your personal or professional life**, leaders and parents need to define the few things they need to ensure strategic consistency in their family, department, or organization. Be clear on what is required to be strategically consistent, such as your core values and beliefs, your ideal shared vision, and key strategies.

▶ In addition, most organizations need strategic consistency only in the following few areas:

- ■ Financial Arrangements
- ■ Management/Succession Planning
- ■ Organization Identity and Visibility/Positioning

- Beyond these few strategic consistencies, operational flexibility and empowerment should reign for all employees once they are given the proper training and tools.

- **In your personal life**, find tolerance for other family members, friends, and colleagues. Allow them the flexibility to live their lives as they want, as long as they stay true to the agreed upon family values.

▶ **For children**, specify as few rules as possible but adhere to them with integrity and consistency.

TOOL #7 SUMMARY

Delegate and empower the "means" to those closest to the task.

But first, ensure clarity and agreement on outcomes (the "ends").

Worksheet #7

I. At Work

In your work environment, what are the few things that are required to be strategically consistent?

Core Values:	Vision/Core Strategies:
1. _____	1. _____
2. _____	2. _____
3. _____	3. _____
4. _____	4. _____
5. _____	5. _____
6. _____	6. _____
7. _____	7. _____

II. At Play & Life

In regards to your personal life, what are those few key kinds of integrity issues that you don't allow people in your life to cross unrestricted? List them here:

1. _____

2. _____

3. _____

4. _____

5. _____

6. _____

7. _____

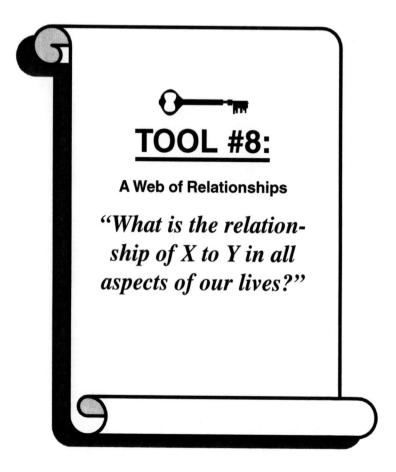

TOOL #8:

A Web of Relationships

"What is the relationship of X to Y in all aspects of our lives?"

The World is Inter-Connected

(and not just through the Internet)

TOOL #8: A Web of Relationships

> **Systems Question:**
> *"What is the relationship of X to Y in all aspects of our lives?"*

The basic definition of a system is two or more related components that work together in support of the whole. If there is no relationship, it is not a system.

Since individuals, families, departments, organizations, and communities are living systems, all of their parts are related (to a greater or lesser extent). You must always look at the relationship of the parts to both:

1. The overall system outcomes
2. All other parts within the living system

■ **In systems, the whole is primary and the parts are secondary.** And the parts are only important within their relationship to other parts and events that support the desired outcomes.

■ **The keys are balance and optimization**, not dominance and maximization of a single part, department, or person.

■ In systems, relationships and processes are what's important, not departments or events.

 **PRINCIPLE**

Change your thinking:
From events and parts
To relationships and processes.

Life is a **"Web of Relationships"**

PRINCIPLE

The whole is more than the sum of the parts. The web of relationships is key.

The most important assessment for any living system (such as families or organizations) is to examine the parts. However, be sure they are linked in an integrated fashion, in support of the desired outcomes.

Analysis of each parts' effectiveness cannot be analyzed in a void, but only in relationship to the other parts and related to the objectives of the whole system.

▶ *Always remember, a system cannot be subdivided into independent parts.*

A change in one part affects both the outcomes and the other webs of interdependent parts or processes. This is true whether talking about families, teams, departments, neighborhoods, organizations, or society as a whole.

EXAMPLE

▶ In organizations, it's not "how can I maximize my job or department's impact?" It's "how can we all work and fit together in support of the overall objectives of the organization?"

To that end, each year all major departments need to share (and have critiqued) their annual plans, with a critical mass of managers or professionals to ensure everyone knows what everyone else is doing. This process is actually a large team-building experience.

EXAMPLES

▶ **Personally,** Systems Thinking is finding patterns and relationships in your work and your life—and learning to reinforce or change these patterns to achieve personal fulfillment. This can actually help to simplify life as you see its interconnections.

▶ What is the relationship between your level of fitness and your energy, overall feelings of health, and stamina to do your job and run your life each day?

USES

▶ **The Interdependence Paradigm:** "We are all **interdependent** with each other." We all know that we are a part of a vast, interrelated universe—ever since the astronaut pictures of earth came back from space.

▶ Why don't you focus on the interrelatedness of key people in our lives and our relationships with them? On a continuing and regular basis, look at the desired outcomes, visions, and purposes you have that affect others: it is key to share and agree on these visions together; and gaining feedback on this vision and your part in it.

▶ Pay close attention to the impact you have on others and they on you. Rarely do you really know the full impact of your actions on others.

▶ Keep asking this Systems Question: *What is the relationship of X to Y* in all aspects of life?

Create "synergy" in your life. Synergy is the working together of two or more parts of any system to produce an effect greater than the sum of the individual effects. It is increasing your own outcomes by working together with others using a more effective, win-win strategy.

The Either/Or Corollary

Either/or questions (X vs Y) usually should be answered by "yes, both" since there are usually multiple causes and multiple effects or outcomes related to most issues.

▶ *Watch out for this trap!*

Forget the artificial and analytic "tyranny of the either/or" question with one-right-answer, and evolve to the Systems Thinking "genius."

Genius of the "and"—the ability to embrace two or more different opinions, extremes, or seemingly contradictory statements at any one time. That is why one can see social problems as a puzzle.

○━━₸

Social Problems as a Puzzle

"A puzzle is a problem that we usually cannot
solve because we make an incorrect
assumption or self-imposed constraint that
precludes solution."

—*Russ Ackoff*

EXAMPLE

▶ When someone asks, "Is it **X** or **Y**?" this is often based on an incorrect assumption: that there is only one right answer.

This happens in organizations, families, and all interpersonal relationships—often resulting in needless conflict, differences of opinions, and hard feelings.

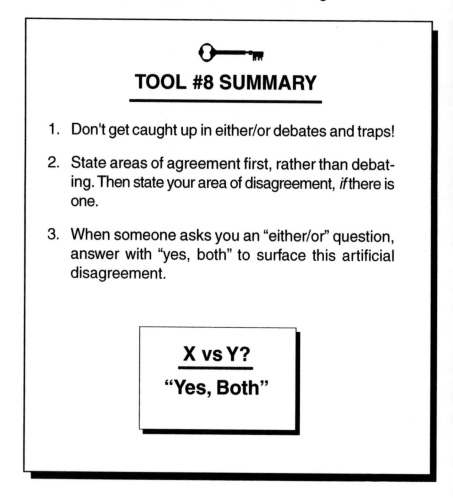

TOOL #8 SUMMARY

1. Don't get caught up in either/or debates and traps!

2. State areas of agreement first, rather than debating. Then state your area of disagreement, *if* there is one.

3. When someone asks you an "either/or" question, answer with "yes, both" to surface this artificial disagreement.

X vs Y?
"Yes, Both"

Worksheet #8

I. At Work

A) Think of a project you are working on now. List it below:

_____

_____

B) Now, think through "who else to involve" in your project, why, and how to do it?

Who to involve?	Why?	How?
1.		
2.		
3.		

II. At Play & Life

A) Is there anyone in your entire life (including people at work) who constantly asks you "X vs Y" Questions? List here:

_____

B) List at least three ways you can stop this downward spiral of artificial "either/or" traps:

1.	
2.	
3.	

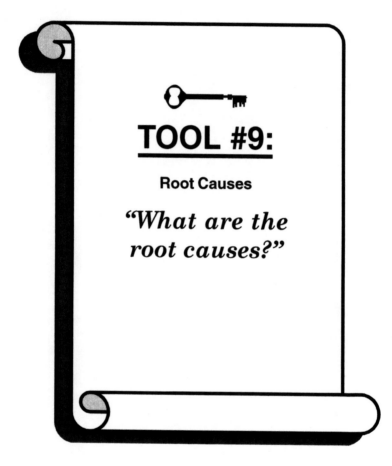

TOOL #9:

Root Causes

"What are the root causes?"

TOOL #9: Root Causes

> **Systems Question:**
>
> *"What are the root causes?"*

We often do not realize the impact we have on others. **The relationship between different parts of a complex system are usually difficult to define,** much less understand. In addition, decisions made in the past often impact results (or lack thereof) today. Thus, it helps to use free-flowing and participative management techniques to find linkages. These strategies reveal the multiple causality factors that are *really* the root causes.

Your actions each day have a long-term impact on others.

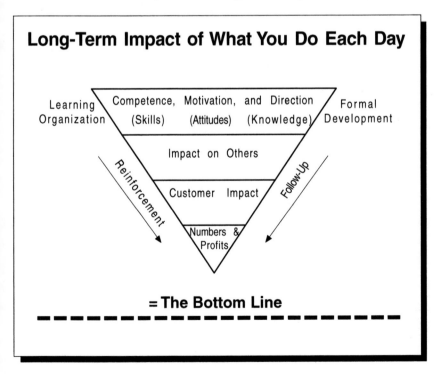

Long-Term Impact of What You Do Each Day

Learning Organization

Competence, Motivation, and Direction

(Skills) (Attitudes) (Knowledge)

Formal Development

Impact on Others

Reinforcement

Customer Impact

Follow-Up

Numbers & Profits

= The Bottom Line

Look deeply for the Root Causes!

PRINCIPLE

While Root Causes are usually not linked closely in time and space— their effects can be far reaching.

Our simplistic "cause and effect" analyses and desire for quick fixes often *create* more problems than they solve. Because our world (earth) is composed of seven levels of complex and interdependent living systems, **multiple causes with multiple effects are our true reality**.

For example, our local weather and crops are affected by the ocean, clouds, rain, wind, plants, and food (i.e., El Nino).

Delay time—the time between causes and their impacts— can have an enormous influence on a system. The concept of "delayed effect" is often missed in our impatient society. It is often too subtle, ignored, and almost always underestimated. When we feel that results aren't happening quickly enough, it shakes our confidence, unnecessarily causing violent "knee-jerk" reactions.

Decisions often have long-term consequences years later. Mind mapping, fishbone diagrams, and all sorts of creativity and brainstorming tools can be used to project consequences.

However, *keep in mind that an issue's complexity often extends far beyond our human ability to fully assess and comprehend the consequences intuitively.* For this reason, it is crucial to flag or anticipate obstacles, understand and appreciate them, and learn to work *with* them rather than against them.

It takes a team effort, too!

EXAMPLES

▶ If you are relatively new in your organization, do you know its history and why some things are the way they are? Ask around and learn them. Remember, *"Things are the way they are because someone wanted them that way."*

▶ If someone makes a decision in your life that affects you but doesn't make sense to you, ask the person the rationale for their decision. Then, ask them again, "Is there any other reason?" Ask it a third time to get at the *real* reason he/she have this view.

▶ When you are about to make a major decision in your life or your work, stop and "troubleshoot" the decision prior to implementing it. For example, ask who it might impact, positively or negatively. Then check with that person about it.

⚴ TOOL #9 SUMMARY

1. Involve people affected by a change in the search for root causes and solutions.

2. To find the root causes, the training and development function has many active learning techniques.

3. Use these active learning techniques to search for root causes vs. "surface symptoms." Some root causes are very hard to find.

4. Continually ask, *"What else might be the root causes?"*

5. Keep an open systems view of the environment, as it often contributes to the overall root causes.

Worksheet #9

I. At Work

What is one problem you have had a difficult time solving at work? List it here: _____

_____

A) What are three reasons why this might still be in existence?

1. _____

2. _____

3. _____

B) What are three more reasons (Root Causes) this might still be unresolved?

1. _____

2. _____

3. _____

II. At Play & Life

What is one problem you have had a difficult time solving in your life? List it here: _____

_____

A) What are three reasons why this might still be in existence?

1. _____

2. _____

3. _____

B) What are three more reasons (Root Causes) this might still be unresolved?

1. _____

2. _____

3. _____

TOOL #10:

Simplicity

"How can we go from complexity to simplicity in the solutions we devise?"

TOOL #10: Simplicity

Systems Question

"How can we go from complexity to simplicity and from consistency to flexibility in the solutions we devise?"

Flexibility, looseness, adaptiveness, speed, and KISS (simplicity) concepts are much more important today in the 21st Century than rigid plans, tight controls, one-size-fits-all consistently, and economies of scale.

We need to eliminate the waste of complexity, bureaucracy, hierarchy, and extra levels in every system. Bureaucracy has run amuck in our lives and can be very harmful.

PRINCIPLE

Make it Your Goal to:
Simplify, Simplify, Simplify!

Systems upon systems are too complex to fully understand and manage centrally, so we must constantly strive to simplify our lives and work.

In understanding the complexities of systems, liberation from regulation and the formation of smaller units is generally more efficient for corporate bureaucracies, privatization, and free market economies than government or big business can ever be.

It is the thousands and thousands of little decisions we all make daily in our businesses that shape and meet these market needs—not central government regulations. Clearly, government has a role to play in today's society, just not an all-encompassing one! The same is true for big corporations.

Enjoy the simplicity of a sunset!

We need to eliminate the waste that complexity brings. The KISS method is more powerful than many economies of scale.

Focus on the fundamentals, *not* **the fads.** In the future, the virtual corporation may very well be more effective than the more traditional, vertically-integrated, complex organization.

Three Magic Questions to Build in Simplicity

1. What kind of simplicity sleuth team should be set up?
2. What are the abrasive or problem areas in the organization or my personal life that should be examined?
3. If you could change the organization or your life with a "stroke of the pen," what would you do?

EXAMPLE

▶ **Rule of 3**
Four leaf clovers are a rarity and, many believe, good luck. The world mostly operates from the "Rule of Three"—beginning, middle, end; sun, moon, stars; body, mind, spirit; air, land, water. In fact, this method of reducing and seeing the world in three is the key to the KISS Method (Keep It Simple, Sweetheart).

"Life's Rules of 3"			
Application	**1**	**2**	**3**
Individuals	Body	Mind	Spirit
Learning	Skills	Knowledge	Feelings/ Attitude
Human Interactions	Structure	Content	Process

▶ *Management's Ultimate Challenge: Search for the simplicity on the far side of complexity.*

"I wouldn't give a fig for the simplicity this side of complexity
but
I'd give my life for the simplicity on the far side of complexity."
—*Justice Oliver Wendell Holmes*

"Any idiot can simplify by ignoring the complications,
but
it takes real genius to simplify by including the complications."

—*John E. Johnson, TEC Chair (The Executive Committee)*

☉━🗝
TOOL #10 SUMMARY

1. When giving a talk or a presentation—in fact, whenever you are trying to influence someone—*reduce your views to three main points*. Everyone will remember them more easily.

3. When someone else is being complex or rambling on, ask them for their three main points or responses.

4. Ask people to analyze any situation with their three *pro* points and three *con* points on an issue.

5. Let's also make a rule that anything we can't explain in three minutes or three sentences is too complex.

6. Summarize an issue or solution on one piece of paper.

Worksheet #10

I. At Work

Ten ways to reduce bureaucracy (and create simplicity and more flexibility)

In terms of your own job or career, answer these questions:

1. What made me mad today? _____
2. What took too long? _____
3. What was the cause of any complaints? _____
4. What was misunderstood? _____
5. What cost too much? _____
6. What was wanted? _____
7. What was too complicated? _____
8. What was just plain silly? _____
9. What job took too many people? _____
10. What job involved too many actions? _____

II. At Play & Life

Ten ways to reduce bureaucracy (and create simplicity and more flexibility)

In terms of your own life, answer these questions:

1. What made me mad today? _____
2. What took too long? _____
3. What was the cause of any complaints? _____
4. What was misunderstood? _____
5. What cost too much? _____
6. What was wanted? _____
7. What was too complicated? _____
8. What was just plain silly? _____
9. What job took too many people? _____
10. What job involved too many actions? _____

The Simplicity of Systems Thinking

"For **EVERYDAY** *Use at Work and Play"*

SECTION IV:

Information

The Top 10 EVERYDAY Tools

From

Systems Thinking

Stephen Haines

CENTRE for STRATEGIC MANAGEMENT®

About the Centre

The Centre for Strategic Management® is an unusual mix of 13 master level consultants as Partners and Affiliates across North America. We also have a growing number of master consultants around the globe.

OUR MISSION

▶ We enhance the strategic management and leadership capabilities of senior executives, their teams, and their organizations in the private, public, and not-for-profit sectors.

▶ We customize **The Systems Thinking Approach**SM with each client to facilitate the development and practical implementation of a tailored Strategic Management System.

▶ We enable clients to create and sustain a customer-focused high performance organization, which is their true competitive advantage within our world of continual change.

OUR CORE VALUES

We at the Centre conduct our lives, our business, and our decision-making as colleagues through:

Integrity and Transparency – in all our relationships.

Service to Others – by sharing our talents to make a difference.

Professionalism & Teamwork – as master level professionals.

Flexibility and Loose-Tight Relationships – of inter- independence.

Respect and Trust – and value the uniqueness of others.

Caring and Abundance – by support for others.

Systems Thinking – as a wholistic and elegantly simplistic approach to life.

Balance and Harmony – in body, mind, and spirit.

OUR VISION

▶ We are a leading-edge international alliance of diverse master consultants, who are recognized and sought after for our unique Systems Thinking Approach[SM] to Strategic Management… our only business.

▶ We are free to pursue our individual and collective passions for our work with clients, while collaborating to create value and wealth for our clients and one another.

▶ This new orientation to life makes a significant difference in our own lives, the lives of senior executives and their organizations, and the communities and societies in which we live and work.

OUR FULLY INTEGRATED LINES OF BUSINESS

1. **The Strategic Edge**—Creation of a Strategic Management System: Strategic Planning, Business Planning, and Change Management.

2. **The People Edge**—Attunement with People's Hearts and Minds: Leadership Development, Strategic Human Resource Management, and Executive Coaching and Team Building.

3. **The Customer Edge**—Alignment of Delivery: Organization Design and Restructuring, Process Redesign, Strategic Marketing and Positioning.

4. **The Systems Thinking Approach**[SM]—Our Foundation: Systems Thinking, Adult Learning, Group Facilitation, and Innovation.

About the Author

Stephen Haines

"CEO, Entrepreneur and Strategist ...

Facilitator, Systems Thinker and Author"

Stephen Haines has used Systems Thinking as his orientation to life since the late 1970s. He is now President and Founder of the Centre for Strategic Management.® He is an internationally recognized leader in the Systems Thinking Approach℠ as applied to strategic management (planning, change, leadership, innovation, and process improvement) to create customer value. He has over 25 years of diverse international executive and consultant experience in virtually every part of the private and public sectors.

Steve was formerly president and part owner of University Associates (UA) Consulting and Training Services. Prior to that, he was Executive Vice President and Chief Administrative Officer of Imperial Corporation of America, a $13 billion nationwide financial services firm. He has been on eight top management teams with organization leadership for operations, planning, human resources, training, organization development, marketing, sales, communications, public relations, and facilities.

A 1968 U.S. Naval Academy Engineering graduate (at Annapolis, MD) with a foreign affairs minor, Steve has an Ed. D. (ABD) in management and educational psychology from Temple University and a Master of Science in Organization Development with a minor in finance from George Washington University.

Steve has published eight books and also written eight volumes of the Centre's Tool Kits, Guides and Best Practices (over 4000 pages) all based on The Systems Thinking Approach℠. He has taught over 60 different type seminars and is in demand as a keynote speaker on CEO and Board of Director's issues. He has served on a number of boards and was chairman of the board for Central Credit Union in San Diego.

Steve can be e-mailed at <u>stephen@csmintl.com</u> at our San Diego Headquarters.

How To Order

Date _____ If Rush Order, need products by _____

Name _____ Title _____

Company _____

Shipping Address _____

City _____ State/Province _____

Country _____ Zip/Postal Code _____

Phone _____ Fax _____ Email _____

Qty.	Code	Description	Price	Amount
	HB-2	Top 10 Tools from Systems Thinking	$9.95	

QTY. DISCOUNTS:
Handbook #2

1-99 copies = $9.95 ea.	Sub total
100-999 copies = $9.50 ea.	Sales Tax (CA residents only)
1000-4999 copies = $9.25 ea.	Shipping/handling charges (min. $5.00—we will complete)
5000+ copies = $9.00 ea.	**TOTAL** (*payable in U.S.$*)

TO ORDER

SYSTEMS THINKING PRESS®

Mail: 5119 Crown Street, San Diego, CA 92110-1511 USA

Phone: (619) 275-6528 or (800) 266-6744

Fax: (619) 275-0324 (24 hours per day, 7 days per week)

Email: info@systemsthinkingpress.com

WWW   Website: www.systemsthinkingpress.com